Life in Poetry

ELIZA ROJAS

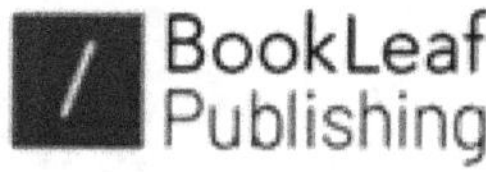

Presentation by *BookLeaf Publishing*

Web: www.bookleafpub.com

E-mail: info@bookleafpub.com

ISBN : 9789357210973

First edition 2022

DEDICATION

To my children, Aleya and Muhammed. I love you two very much, and I hope one day when you are old enough to read and perhaps much older you will be proud of me and know that I truly enjoy writing. I love writing poetry and I love telling my life story. To my mother, I love you very much and want to tell you that you are the best mother in the world, and I could never imagine my life without you. Thank you for everything you have done for myself and my siblings. Thank you Lana, for providing my family with a home for years, you didn't have to, but you wanted to, thank you. Love you. Lastly, I want to think God, because without him, I wouldn't be where I am at, creating this poem book.

ACKNOWLEDGEMENT

I would like to thank BookLeafPublishing for giving me the opportunity to create this book with such a small amount to pay forward. This is truly a blessing!

PREFACE

This book came into being because I wanted to create something memorable that would describe every day life and things. I also wanted to incorporate personal life events that have happened in my life, as a child and as an adult. The last 5 poems are random everyday life poems, the other 16 are actually life events that I have experienced. I hope that whomever gets their hand on this book, is able to feel my poetry. When I write, I do it from the heart. I also love to ryhme with my poems, almost identical to freestyling.

His Infidelity

It got me by surprise
One moment life was good, living happily
Until all that died.
I felt like I was being swallowed by all the lies.
When will he come home?
His phone keeps ringing, he's not even
answering messages,
How do I even know if he is alone?
I just don't know.
But he tells me he loves me,
That nobody will get in between us,
But that's not what I see,
I can't help but think all these negative things,
About the woman he's been with,
How enjoyable it must be for her
To be with him,
The feeling of being intimate.
And when he talks to me after he's done with
her,
He's always so happy,
A happy glow in his eyes,
Is all I can see,
Maybe one day I will be enough for him
And he can choose me,
Over that woman,

I can forgive, but I will never forget.
My empty heart will forever ache,
the feeling of infidelity,
his infidelity.

First Love

Was it a crush, was it puppy love, or was it true
love?
I had met my first boyfriend,
Very unexpected.
I was not even interested.
You were a bad boy, and I was a good girl
You were "too spicy" for me,
Yet I didn't really care.
The feeling of vulnerability,
love was in the air.
Just 2 young lovers falling in love.
Destiny had brought us together,
To cross each other's path,
I can't deny I was truly sprung,
I knew I loved you since the start.
You were like a knight in shining armour for me,
You were the only one whom I wanted to be,
with,
I knew my mom wouldn't agree,
That you smoked weed,
A true weed fiend.
Since you started smoking at the age of eight.
I don't even know who accepted,
To be your plug,
It's crazy to me!

I tried to change you,
I was hoping you would quit smoking.
But I quickly realized, it was a part of you.
The man you wanted to be,
But those times that cops were involved,
We were all in danger.
I didn't want you to get caught
I ignored all the red flags,
That came with you,
We were two young lovers,
With a new beginning,
Hoping for a beautiful, future.
You were my first boyfriend ever,
And you were to later become my husband,
Then I went into the service, my best friend,
And our marriage life began.
We were always together,
Through the very thick and thin,
It was a beautiful love story,
Our love was truly magical.
I felt like a pretty princess, living in a fairytale.
But the difference was,
That our love was true.
I knew, you knew,
that I always loved you.

Single Mom Life

Every morning I get up,
And I snooze my alarm,
I am way too tired to look at the time,
But some how I manage to push a button,
And go back to bed.
But then I get up at 4:30 in the morning,
I prepare everything for the day,
Dress Muhammed,
And go straight to work,
After taking my baby to daycare,
I'm always in a hurry,
With a million things to do.
I don't even know how I manage to eat everyday,
Since I don't like to cook,
The life of a single mom.
The hardest life I've had.
I never thought,
This is what my mom,
went through,
To take care of all of us siblings,
I knew she had to have had a breakthrough,
With her not having any help,
from my sperm donor.
My father.

I feel like I never have enough time to do what I
need to do.
As I am always on the go,
But I know,
being a single mama is by far the hardest thing
I've done.
I just want my children healthy, loving and
smart.
My ultimate goal as a mom,
Single mom life is kinda very hard.
But I'll never take the easy way out,
With a hand by my side, a hand holding my
child,
I know there's no discontinue,
It's only a small phase of a chapter,
Single mom life,
is another challenge,
I have encountered.
I would not trade being a mom,
Like NEVER.
I made my bed,
So I now must lay in it.
To my children,
I love you.
I'll be both the mommy and daddy If I have to,
Single mom life isn't for the weak,
But dear God,
to my beautiful , and amazing children,
I love being a mother!

Homelessness

The feeling of not having a home,
Was the worst thing,
I remember the first day we lost our home,
My mother hadn't worked in years,
Her pockets were empty.
We were all alone.
The money my stepfather would give her
weekly,
Just wasn't enough.
It was only enough to eat,
The feeling of being homeless was inevitable.
So my sister,
And her boyfriend took us in their home.
Six people in their house must have been a
miracle.
To think we had been homeless,
Until they took us in.
We will never forget this journey.
Truly devastating,
But we cannot control our destiny,
And may we never again be homeless.

To my Son

Son,
You are the best man in my life,
When you were born,
I knew you would be special.
You saved my life.
 I was in a very bad moment when you were
born.
I was confident in my plans, yes,
But I didn't really know,
if that was truly the way to go.
I knew you were the missing piece.
Though I already had your sister,
I needed a little king in my life,
To toughen me up.
A little boy,
To make my life better,
Everything about you is so special,
From your brown skin,
to your curly hair,
Your little chubby legs,
Kicking everywhere,
Daddy says you will one day be a soccer player,
From the moment you were born,
I knew,

how truly special you were!
Son, I want you to know,
I will always be there for you,
I will be beside you,
If you need me too,
You can count on me,
For my kids I'll do anything,
Little boy, you are my life.
A little king, has truly blessed me.
When you came to this world,
I didn't know,
That you would take my heart away,
I guess its 100% true,
When they say,
That a son is a woman's first love,
I find that to be completely true.
When I stare at you,
I see a beautiful baby boy slowly growing,
You laugh at everything,
Even when I make the silliest faces.
You are the most beautiful little brown baby boy.
The joy,
You bring to everyone you meet is unreal,
From your beautiful silky skin,
to the curlies, the chubby cheeks,
to your stinky feet.
Boy you have changed my whole life.
I am beyond blessed, to be your mother.
I love you!

The Lies

I had to really figure out,
when you were lying.
Your character was so strong.
 I couldn't tell.
But one day I figured it out,
I had to look through your soul,
Only then I could know,
What emotions and feelings you didn't show,
Your face expressions would give the lies away.
You never would look at me in the face.
Afraid I could tell when you lied,
Because you didn't wanna be known as fake,
But you really knew how to hide things.
Although I could tell,
I would use my sensing.
Why couldn't you just be truthful to me,
I loved you unconditionally.
I wonder if she treated you better than me.
And she gave you what you needed,
Because you didn't have me,
I believed you, because I loved you,
I knew about the lies,
But you were far away from me,
I had no choice,
but to let you be.

God Forgive Me

God forgive me for every sin I've done,
You know my life,
I have truly screwed up,
Many times thinking something was for me,
When red flags showed, clearly not,
God forgive me for everything I am,
and for the woman I am not.
Because of you I have strength, to move
forward.
I know looking back is not ideal,
So I must always look up towards my future.
God forgive me for being so rebellious, when I
should have been grounded.
For thinking that I can do whatever I want,
without repercussion,
God forgive me,
For being warned to stay away
from certain people.
I just couldn't see,
the future.
God forgive me,
for at times not being the best version of myself,
I knew you were watching me,
Throughout my journey,
I'm sorry if you thought I wasn't listening,

Please God,
Forgive me.

Little Girl

Little girl afraid of being alone,
Her stepfather always wants to strike her,
Her mother always has to leave for work,
And the little girl stays at home,
Crying her eyes out feeling so alone,
Afraid to tell her mother,
Because she thinks she wont believe her,
Her mother is in love with her stepfather, this
she knows.
Little girl hiding behind a living room cabinet,
She hides away in hopes that her stepfather
doesn't know where she's located,
But this is an easy skill he now has,
he immediately finds her location.
Little girl, her face full in tears follows the yank
of her stepfather who takes her away,
Leads her to the bedroom,
And touches her all over,
He doesn't have regret or remorse,
he just knows,
Little girl is way too young to tell her mother
she was abused,
After everything is done, the stepfather walks
away without a worry,

because the little girl would never tell,
Little girl living in a world of worry,
Every day that her mom goes to work,
She cries, because she doesn't want to be alone.
This man,
wont leave her alone.
And no one knows.

Girl Soldier in Combat

I am a female Soldier,
In my uniform I stand,
With my cap in my head,
And boots in hand,
I am ready to fight,
In air, water, or land,
American Soldier in training,
Marching every morning,
In PT gear, working out.
Through our lungs singing cadence,
Awfully loud,
Back to the bay we go, rushing to shower,
But they don't have much time.
It's time to eat chow,
Military girl,
Going to war,
Training for pre-deployment,
Attending all these classes,
With a duffel bag in hand,
Assault bag in our back,
Dog tags around our necks,
Ready to travel abroad,
Prayers surrounding our energy,
In hopes,

We stay safe,
Away from our enemy.
American Soldier, in the making.
Awaiting, for the time,
It's time to go back home,
Our dearest families,
Awaiting our arrival,
Soon if it will be time to go.

Losing Myself

I never understood what people meant
When they said,
they lost themselves.
Until the day that I myself,
Lost Myself,
I felt deep in love with a man,
Who showed me my worth, and that
I shouldn't take no shit,
He showed me the right way to be treated,
But then things changed,
He folded on me,
I knew when he did,
but he never confessed to me,
As a woman I used my intuition
My gut feeling,
He showed me alot of signs,
But when I would ask him, he always denied,
I knew if I mentioned it,
He would only lie,
I truly lost myself in this situation,
Because I was deeply in love,
I kept asking myself, "what exactly did I do
wrong?"
I couldn't think of anything I had done,
so maybe I wasn't the problem.

I was trapped in my own head ,
Thoughts racing,
everytime I would hang up with him,
I knew about it,
I was still loosing myself deeply,
I even cried myself to sleep, some nights, as I
drunk my favorite whisky.
We told ourselves , if there ever comes a day
where you want to cheat on me,
just tell me, or leave.
We both agreed.
How could he break his promise to me?
I was in complete disbelief,
Something I refused to,
I told myself, I will not lose myself again,
Not for a man,
I told myself if a man can't love you,
the way your'e suppose to be loved,
Move on.
I never wanted to lose myself again.

Female Soldier

I am an American Soldier,
In my uniform I stand,
With my cap in my head,
And boots in hand,
American Soldier in training,
Marching every morning,
In pt gear, working out,
Through our lungs singing cadence,
Awfully loud,
Back to the bay we go, rushing to shower
But they don't have much time,
It's time to eat chow,
American Soldier,
Going to war,
Training for pre-deployment,
Attending all these classes,
With a duffel bag in hand,
Assault bag in our back,
Dog tags around our necks,
Ready to travel abroad,
Prayers surrounding our energy,
In hopes,
We stay safe,
Away from our enemy.
American Soldier, in the making.

Awaiting for the time,
In which it is time to go back home!!
Our dearest families,
Awaiting our arrival,
Soon it will be time to go.

End Racism

Every day we all get up in the morning the same
way,
We put on our big boy pants and then go about
our day.
With this in mind, we should be able to say,
that racism has died.
Because even though our skin may be a different
pigment.
Every day we wake up in the morning, and do
our own routines.
Racism in this world,
is still very much existent,
I pray that when my children go to school,
racism wont be introduced to them,
But I know better than to think that so fast it
ends.
I truly can't wait for the day,
Where I do not have to think about being talked
about because my skin is different,
But for what reason?
We all bleed the same color,
And we are all just human,
While I am not scared of hardly anything,
I put myself in those people's shoes,
Knowing what they've gone through,

Though I am brown skinned,
And I have my hispanic culture running
through my veins.
And actually,
I have had racist remarks , thrown at me
By my close friends even,
But flesh is always the same color
I look forward for the day,
that everyone can come together, ignore the
pigment,
The color,
And love one another.

Father

Father,
Though I've never really met you,
Only a couple times in jail did I see you,
I want you to know,
that I am here.
I have forgiven you, but don't think I can ever
forget.
The thought of my mama being left out in the
cold.
Taking care of children, all on her own.
You didn't really support her,
When she needed you the most,
That's what really hurts.
Father, I wish things would have been different,
and you could've been there for your children,
But you chose the streets, and your bummy
friends.
Though I am not here to judge you,
Because I know you were only growing up,
Committing petty crime, smoking, and maybe
even getting drunk.
I want you to know that your children still want
to see you.
Well atleast I do,
I would like to see you atleast once.

cause after all, you're still my biological dad.

The Beautiful Ones are Not Yet Born

The act of life itself is the most beautiful thing to
happen,
Out of life comes a beautiful human,
In the new beginning of a new era,
You see the world is not necessarily the nicest
place to be,
It's full of jealousy, crime, political proganda,
war, judgement, and full of cruelty.
Through learning how the world works,
I have observed,
What I now know,
how the beautiful ones are not yet born.

How Can You?

How can you say to me that you love me,
And still have sex with her?
Call me beautiful words, like "beautiful" or
"queen"
When you spend the night making love to her,
But I'm not allowed to do the same,
Because it's "nasty"
You're a narcissist,
I never thought that you would play me like a
game,
The worst part is, you lie so good,
You will never confess yourself,
The world could be crashing down,
But your truth lies within yourself,
How can you look at me in the eyes, and still
have feelings for me?
When your lips and hands are not caressing my
body,
But another woman's,
I mean I have given you everything,
I can't understand,
Do you love her?
Who is she?
Does she know about me?
Why don't you ask her for money?

You always tell me, when your in need,
It's like you keep me around you, only to use
me.
How can you play with my feelings, when you
know I'm so emotional,
Tell me you want to marry me, but clearly your
heart and belong to her,
You are literally tearing a whole, right through
my bleeding soul.
You know my past,
What I have been through,
I really thought we could last,
I guess I jumped into this relationship,
Way too fast,
Or maybe not,
See love doesn't have a timer, that states how
many years, how many month's,
You must know the person,
That you love,
How can you say you love me, but make love to
her?
Each night going to sleep early,
because you got work in the morning,
But instead, you have set a schedule for her,
I don't want no more lies, I don't want to hurt
anymore
I need to put myself first,
And realize the truth,
That don't love me, you love her.

Heartbreak

Sometimes we fall deeply in love,
We can be so happy and in love,
Or it may be the wrong one,
We get the butterflies in our stomach.
Our body shakes in embarrassment,
And we just get so nervous,
We have fallen deeply in love with a connection,
And we think, yes this is the one,
The one I love,
So we start dating them,
And learn everything we can for every person,
Now we are super focused,
While for some it is a beautiful love.
For others it's not.
So we ignore every single red flag.
Coming our way.
We don't want to see, what with our own eyes
we can't see
By accepting all these red flags,
We just breaking our own big heart.
The feeling of bad heartbreak,
Ripping our soul apart,
is what it feels like,
Heartbreak is where our love stands.

How We Kiss

I love kissing you,
The way you bite my lips,
And I love your lips, cause
they're so big.
Dark Brown Massive Lips,
I love it, and I melt when,
They touch my lips,
I love the way you kiss,
Next you shift closer to me,
So I can feel your hot body,
Your lips reaching for me,
Your mouth leads my tongue,
in great agony.
Interwining with my lips, a feeling,
I cannot shake,
Cannot resist!
We like to kiss,
Our souls ignite,
with great seduction and passion,
This is how we kiss

Beautiful Butterfly

Beautiful butterfly in the air,
Spread your wings, and fly to me,
Yellow, blue, purple wings.
Flying around beautifully,
Beautiful butterfly fly, fly, fly,
Bringing good luck, in my life,
When you fly around the ponds and the flower
bunches.
A dozen of your beautiful colors flying in all
directions.
Fly, fly, fly beautiful butterfly,
For when the season changes and the weather
warms up,
I shall see you little butterfly,
Looking for your way around,
Your wings flowing, high up in the sky,
Beautiful butterfly, stop being shy,
Where there is beauty and color,
there is life and meaning,
And your beautiful body flies awfully slowly.
Beautiful butterfly, fly, fly, fly, away

A Miracle

When you are lost and have no one to turn to,
Look up,
There is your answer,
God,
Everyone in the world can turn their backs on
you but he will always be there for you.
And that is exactly what I needed to do,
I was at wits end,
I didn't know what career path to take,
My Army contract was about to end,
And I was trying to figure out my next move,
I prayed and told God to guide me, my life is
his,
And he came through,
He showed me a miracle,
I will not say what it was,
Because that's a secret,
But know that I prayed and prayed until I was in
deservance of a beautiful blessing,
Thank you God for everything you have blessed
me with,
A miracle,
I will never forget.

Diego

This poem is dedicated to my dear oldest
brother,
Who passed away in September, 28, 2005,
He was the leader of our pack,
No one could mess with him,
He was a bad ass,
Very well respected,
I remember he was a very hard worker,
He would help my stepfather,
And my stepfather absolutely loved him,
My brother was a problem child,
He would get in so much trouble at school,
But he understood his studies very clear,
The first in his class to answer a question,
The teachers all thought he was so talented,
And smart,
As he was growing up, he would get in trouble
with the law,
One day out of the nowhere my mother got a
call,
Apparently my brother got into trouble,
He was not a legal citizen,
So when he was arrested,
He was also deported,
And they sent him to Mexico,

To start a new life,
For a few years,
Sadly,
those were the longest years of my brother's life,
He was completely depressed, and wanted to
come back home,
He didn't lose hope,
Until one day, he hung himself,
In the roof of where he used to sleep,
In the hard cement,
My brother was a legend,
He is always in our hearts,
And always in our spirit,
Until we meet again,
My brother.

LOVE

34

Love is amazing,
With the right person it is,
Never give up on love.